Theo Gayer-Anderson is a British illustrator and sculptor who lives
in Cairo. Among his works in Egypt he single-handedly carved a
large-scale replica of a pharaonic wall relief. He is the illustrator of
The Legend of Lotfiya, also for Hoopoe Books.

British poet Gerard Benson's collection of poems *Evidence of Elephants*
was nominated for the Carnegie Medal, while his anthology
This Poem Doesn't Rhyme won the Signal Poetry Award.
He lives in England with his wife Cathy and his cat Chivers.

This book was inspired by a reading of *Ozymandias* given by
Gerard Benson during a visit to Cairo.

Ozymandias

Written by
Percy Shelley

Illustrated by
Theo Gayer-Anderson

HOOPOE BOOKS

Percy Shelley's *Ozymandias*

One of my greatest pleasures when I was eight or nine years old was reading. With a book in front of my eyes I could enjoy many adventures. I could encounter unknown lands, both real and imaginary. I liked poems and stories most. Among poems there were a few that stood out from the rest and set my imagination on fire. One was *Tiger* by William Blake. Another was that curious story with lots of made-up words, *Jabberwocky* by Lewis Carroll. Yet another was *Ozymandias*. I didn't know what it was all about, but this traveller's tale of an abandoned and ruined statue, lying in the sands, opened my mind to ideas I hadn't before dreamed of.

I know now that the poem is a sonnet, that the shattered statue was of the pharaoh Rameses the Second and that the poet who wrote it, Percy Bysshe Shelley, died in 1822 at the age of 29. But then, I knew none of this. I didn't even know that the 'antique land' was Egypt.

The rhythm and sound of the language though, and the strange and beautiful name, Ozymandias, held me captive. I read it again and again and imagined the 'lone and level sands' stretching far away while the traveller gazed at the remains of the sculpture of a once-mighty ruler.

In the early 19th century the rest of the world became curious about Egypt. There was a great trade in Egyptian antiquities. Practically every traveller who visited the Nile went off with some object or other. But for some, including Giovanni Belzoni, this was done on a grand scale. Many of these pieces found their way into the private collections and public museums of Europe.

It was in the British Museum in 1817 that Shelley first saw some of these, including a giant statue of Rameses the Second brought to England by Belzoni. Like many British people, Shelley was enchanted. To Europeans at that time, Egypt was a country of infinite mystery, a land of extraordinary temples, jewellery, mummies, obelisks and pyramids; a land of myth; a country which had given birth to one of the world's greatest civilisations.

Shelley, with his friend Horace Smith, decided that they must both write a poem about Egypt. Smith's poem was quite ordinary, but Shelley's was *Ozymandias*. Months later, in February 1818, Shelley again wrote about Egypt. He and his friends Leigh Hunt and John Keats held a competition among themselves. Who could write the best sonnet about the Nile? Hunt's poem won. It began, 'It flows through old hushed Egypt and its sands,' and it shows the awe in which one of the world's greatest rivers was held. And the mystery. After all, the Nile's source was still unknown.

All the same, Shelley's sonnet *Ozymandias* still stands alone. But what *is* a sonnet? Sonnets are poems of fourteen lines, with ten syllables to a line in a 'heartbeat' rhythm. They deal with a single idea. They usually rhyme in a strict pattern; but Shelley has adapted this a little. They have been popular with English poets for over 500 years.

Now let me leave you to enjoy the book: the pictures and the poem. I wish you all the joy from *Ozymandias* that I got all those years ago (though it wasn't as long ago as Shelley – or Rameses the Second!)

Gerard Benson, England, 1999

I met a traveller

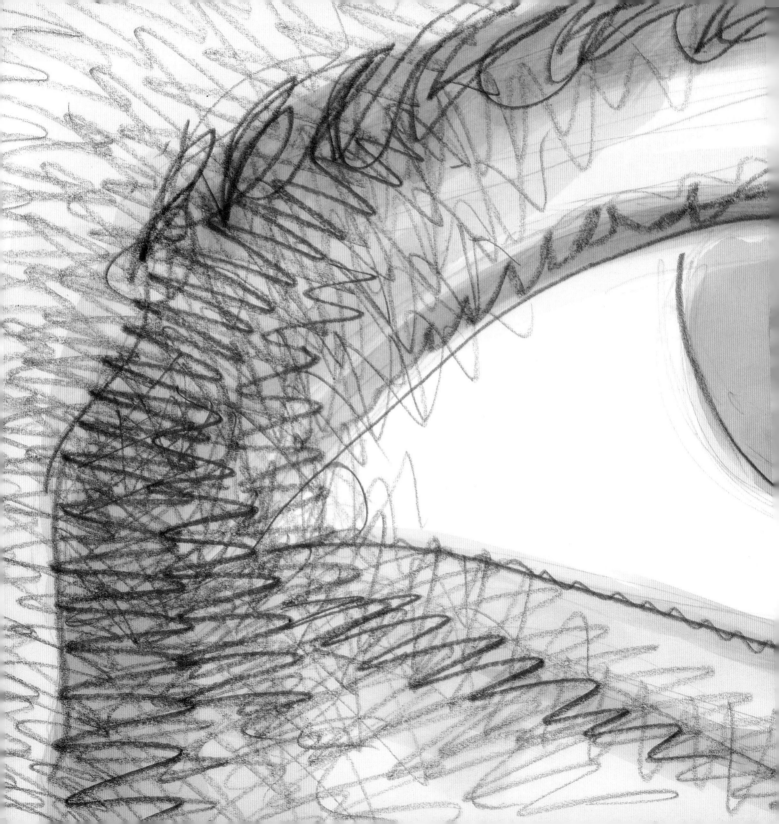

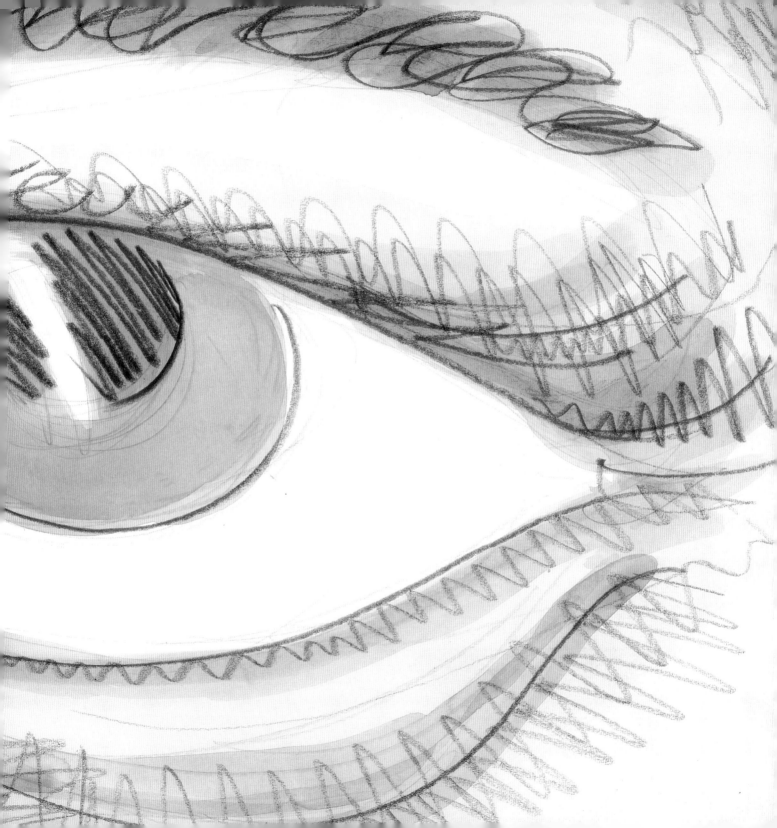

I met a traveller from an antique land
Who said: Two vast and trunkless legs of stone

Stand in the desert . . . Near them, on the sand,
Half sunk, a shattered visage lies, whose frown,

And wrinkled lip, and sneer of cold command,
Tell that its sculptor well those passions read

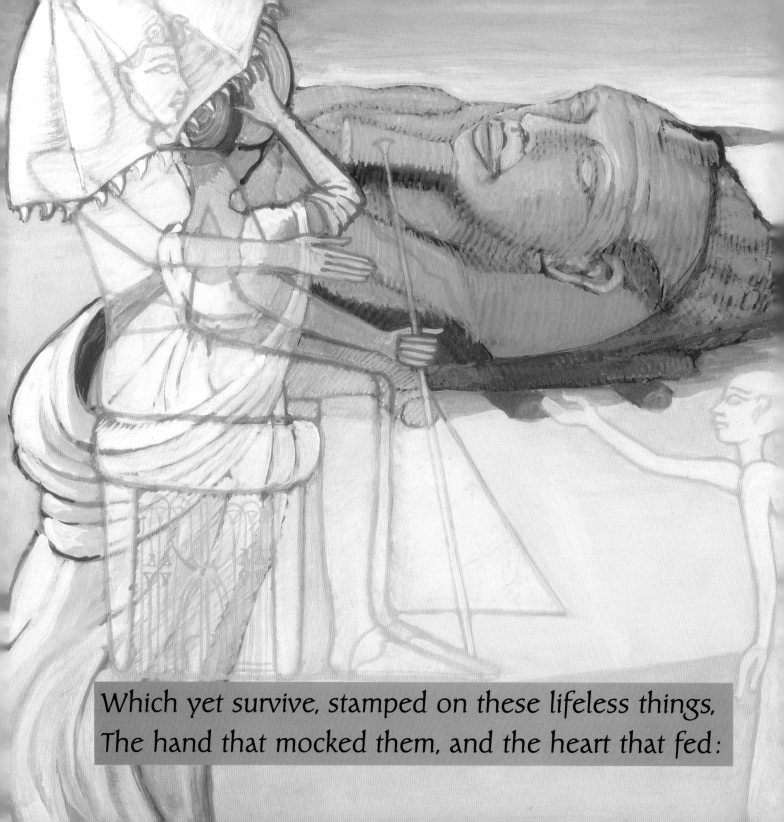

Which yet survive, stamped on these lifeless things,
The hand that mocked them, and the heart that fed:

And on the pedestal these words appear:
'My name is Ozymandias, king of kings:

Look on my works, ye Mighty, and despair!'
Nothing beside remains. Round the decay

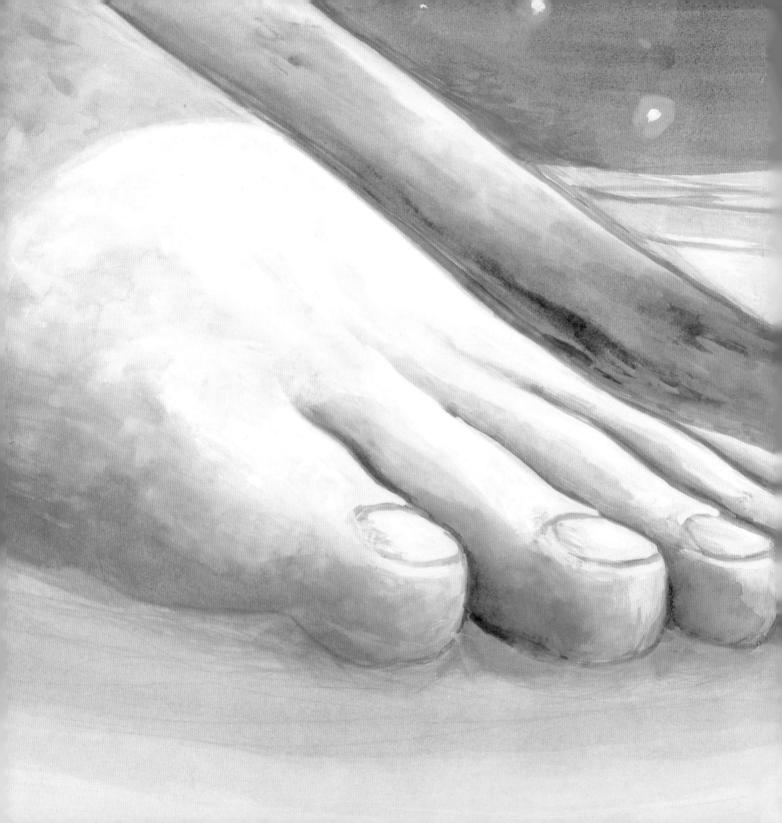

Of that colossal wreck, boundless and bare
The lone and level sands stretch far away.

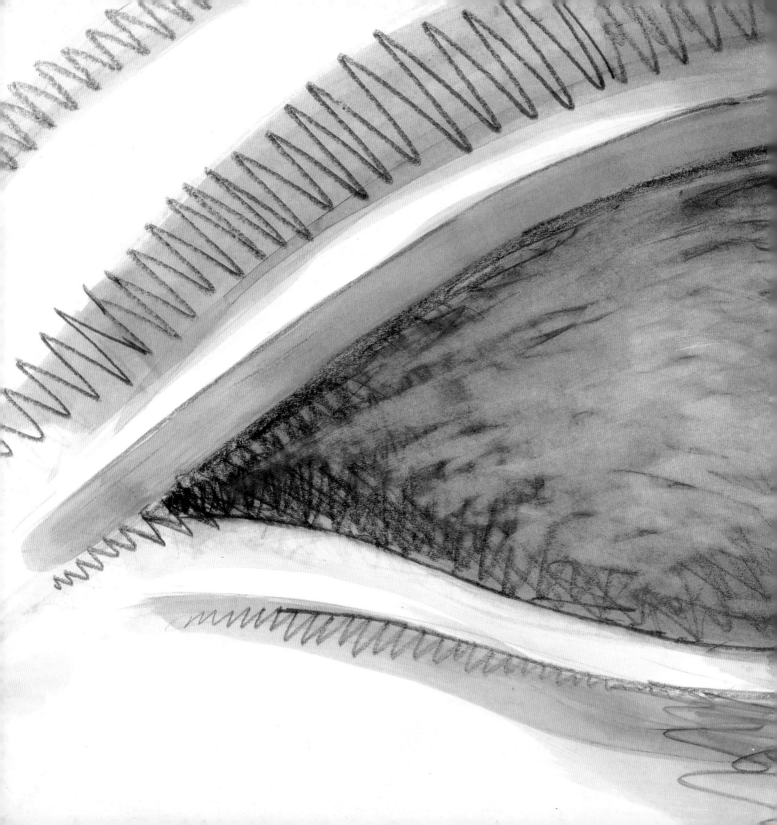

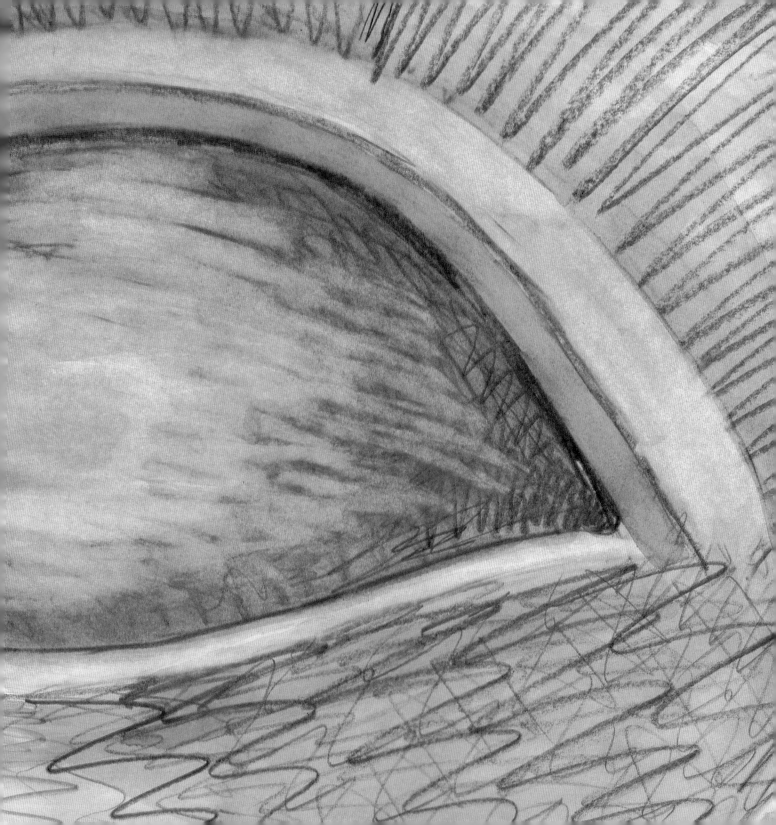

far away

OZYMANDIAS
A POEM
BY PERCY BYSSHE SHELLEY
ILLUSTRATED
BY THEO GAYER-ANDERSON

OZYMANDIAS

I MET A TRAVELLER FROM AN ANTIQUE LAND
WHO SAID: TWO VAST AND TRUNKLESS LEGS OF STONE
STAND IN THE DESERT... NEAR THEM, ON THE SAND,
HALF SUNK, A SHATTERED VISAGE LIES, WHOSE FROWN,
AND WRINKLED LIP, AND SNEER OF COLD COMMAND,
TELL THAT ITS SCULPTOR WELL THOSE PASSIONS READ
WHICH YET SURVIVE, STAMPED ON THESE LIFELESS THINGS,
THE HAND THAT MOCKED THEM, AND THE HEART THAT FED:
AND ON THE PEDESTAL THESE WORDS APPEAR:
'MY NAME IS OZYMANDIAS, KING OF KINGS:
LOOK ON MY WORKS, YE MIGHTY, AND DESPAIR!'
NOTHING BESIDES REMAINS. ROUND THE DECAY
OF THAT COLOSSAL WRECK, BOUNDLESS AND BARE
THE LONE AND LEVEL SANDS STRETCH FAR AWAY.

BEYOND *OZYMANDIAS*
Suggestions for further reading – by Gerard Benson

Shelley and his generation

Many encyclopedias have entries for Percy Bysshe Shelley. Also look for: *Who wrote that? An Instant Guide to Literature*, Terrance Dicks (Red Fox, 1992).

Shelley's other poems are not easily accessible to young readers. However, other poets of Shelley's generation wrote poems that can be enjoyed by all, for example these poems by John Keats (1795–1821): *To Autumn* and *A Song About Myself.*

James Thomson (BV) (1834–82) wrote a poem called *A Voice from the Nile*. The following is an extract from that poem. Thomson called himself BV, meaning 'Bysshe Vanolis', because he admired Shelley so much.

. . . The palm-trees and the doves among the palms,

The corn-fields and the flowers among the corn,

The patient oxen and the crocodiles,

The ibis and the heron and the hawk,

The lotus and the thick papyrus reeds,

The slant-sailed boats that flit before the wind . . .

. . . . . . the massive temple-fronts

With all their columns and huge effigies,

The pyramids and Memnon and the Sphinx,

This Cairo and the city of the Greek . . .

Thomas Lovell Beddoes (1803–49) wrote this wonderful poem called *A Crocodile* when he was just over twenty:

Hard by the lilied Nile I saw
A duskish river-dragon stretched along,
The brown habergeon of his limbs enamelled
With sanguine alamandines and rainy pearl:
And on his back there lay a young one sleeping,
No bigger than a mouse; with eyes like beads,
And a small fragment of its speckled egg
Remaining on its harmless, pulpy snout;
A thing to laugh at, as it gaped to catch
The baulking merry flies. In the iron jaws
Of the great devil-beast, like a pale soul
Fluttering in rocky hell, lightsomely flew
A snowy trochilus, with roseate beak
Tearing the hairy leeches from his throat.

Percy Shelley's wife, Mary Shelley, is almost as well known as her husband. She was the author of the story of *Frankenstein* (1818).

Shelley and Smith's competition

The poem written by Horace Smith (1779–1849) in the competition held for fun with Shelley is on the following page. Its title is rather long, especially when we remember that the title of Shelley's poem was just one word.

On a Stupendous Leg of Granite
Discovered Standing by Itself in the Deserts of Egypt,
with the Inscription inserted below:

In Egypt's sandy silence, all alone,
    Stands a gigantic Leg, which far off throws
    The only shadow that the Desert knows.
'I am great Ozymandias,' saith the stone,
    'The King of Kings; this mighty city shows
The wonders of my hand.' The city's gone!
    Naught but the leg remaining to disclose
The site of that forgotten Babylon.

We wonder, and some hunter may express
Wonder like ours, when through the wilderness
    Where London stood, holding the wolf in chase,
He meets some fragment huge, and stops to guess
    What wonderful, but unrecorded, race
    Once dwelt in that annihilated place.

The statue of Ozymandias

In his poem, Shelley describes the statue as 'colossal'. The word comes from another statue famous in the ancient world, the Colossus. This giant figure was built at the mouth of the harbour of the Greek island of Rhodes and was one of the Seven Wonders of the Ancient World. The Colossus of Rhodes was destroyed in an earthquake.

Illustrations © Theo Gayer-Anderson 1999

First published in 1999 by Hoopoe Books
13 Rashdan Street, Missaha Square, Dokki, Cairo 12311
email: hoopoe@internetegypt.com
website: www.hoopoebooks.com

ISBN 977-5325-82-X
Deposit no: 99/1595

Colour separation by ReproGraphic, Cairo
Printed by Elias Modern Press, Egypt